To my Granddad - Cyril who told us stories

Thanks go to my wife Jo and my girls for encouragement and proof reading. My friend John Bastable for editing, advise and help. And all my friends and family who have encouraged me. And everyone on Instagram who follows, likes and comments.

About the author/illustrator
I live in Brighton with my wife and terrier Hector. A Dad to two wonderful daughters. I'm a bean counter by profession but have always loved to draw and am fascinated by history - this project brings both together.
Tim Catherall May 2023

Instagram @timcatherall
Website www.greatwarpublishing.com
Twitter @greatwarpublish

TRUE TO THEIR SALT

MARSEILLES - SOUTH OF FRANCE LATE SEPTEMBER 1914. A FLEET OF SHIPS HAS SAILED FROM INDIA CARRYING UNITS OF INDIAN EXPEDITIONARY FORCE A COMMANDED BY GENERAL SIR JAMES WILLCOCKS. THEY HAD BEEN SENT BY THE INDIAN GOVERNMENT TO REINFORCE THE HARD PRESSED BRITISH EXPEDITIONARY FORCE (BEF) FIGHTING IN FRANCE. THEY BEGAN LANDING ON 24TH SEPTEMBER AND COMPLETED THE DISEMBARKATION IN EARLY OCTOBER.

THE 7TH MEERUT DIVISION LANDED AT MARSEILLES 12-14 OCTOBER 1914 HAVING BEEN DELAYED BY GERMAN RAIDERS OPERATING IN THE INDIAN OCEAN. ON BOARD WERE THE 58TH VAUGHANS RIFLES (FRONTIER FORCE) AS PART OF THE BAREILLY BRIGADE. AMONGST ITS SOLDIERS WAS JEMADAR (JUNIOR OFFICER) MIR MAST - AN AFRIDI PATHAN FROM THE TRIBAL AREAS OF WHAT IS NOW PAKISTAN.

LOOK BOYS - FRANCE. SOON WE WILL BE AT THE FRONT

THE PEOPLE OF MARSEILLES TURNED OUT TO GREET THE WARRIORS FROM INDIA
WHO HAD COME TO HELP THEM HELP THEM FIGHT THE BOCHE.

THE RACECOURSE JUST OUTSIDE MARSEILLES WAS CHOSEN AS THE SITE FOR THE TROOPS TO REST,
RECUPERATE AND ORGANISE BEFORE HEADING UP NORTH TO THE FRONT LINE.

THE ARMY WAS MINDFUL OF THE VARIOUS CASTES AND
RELIGIONS AND ENSURED THAT COOKING, CLEANING AND
SPIRITUAL NEEDS WERE ALL MET ACCORDING TO THE
VARIOUS CUSTOMS.

THE INDIAN TROOPS WERE ENGENDERED WITH A SPORTING
ÉLAN AND LOVED TO TAKE PART IN FOOTBALL, WRESTLING

AND OF COURSE CRICKET.

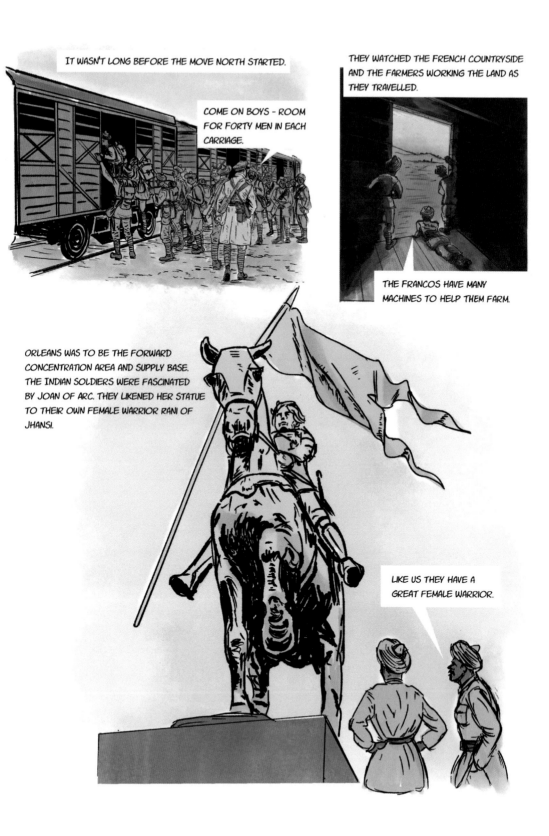

IT WASN'T LONG BEFORE THE MOVE NORTH STARTED.

COME ON BOYS - ROOM FOR FORTY MEN IN EACH CARRIAGE.

THEY WATCHED THE FRENCH COUNTRYSIDE AND THE FARMERS WORKING THE LAND AS THEY TRAVELLED.

THE FRANCOS HAVE MANY MACHINES TO HELP THEM FARM.

ORLEANS WAS TO BE THE FORWARD CONCENTRATION AREA AND SUPPLY BASE. THE INDIAN SOLDIERS WERE FASCINATED BY JOAN OF ARC. THEY LIKENED HER STATUE TO THEIR OWN FEMALE WARRIOR RANI OF JHANSI.

LIKE US THEY HAVE A GREAT FEMALE WARRIOR.

THE SEPOYS WERE SENT TO PARTS OF THE LINE WHERE THEY WERE MOST NEEDED.

THEY MOVED UP TO THE FRONT IN STEPS - FIRSTLY TRANSPORTED IN LONDON BUSES.

AND THEN MARCHING THE LAST FEW MILES.

I CAN HEAR THE GUNS JEMADAR.

WE ARE GETTING CLOSE BOYS.

THE FIRST TRENCHES WERE NOTHING MORE THAN DITCHES.

THE INDIANS INITIALLY TOOK OVER AT A PLACE CALLED WYTSCHAETE IN BELGIUM.

VAUGHAN'S RIFLES ARE DISPATCHED TO REPLACE DISMOUNTED CAVALRY HOLDING THE LINE. THEIR FIRST TOUR OF DUTY WAS RELATIVELY CALM.

IT'S VERY QUIET JEMADAR MAST.

IT WILL SOON HOT UP! BUT WE COULD DO WITH WARMER CLOTHES.

THE INDIANS WERE ISSUED WITH GREATCOATS, PULLOVERS, LONG JOHNS AND BALACLAVAS TO HELP KEEP THEM DRY AND WARM IN THEIR LIGHTER UNIFORMS UNTIL THEY COULD BE ISSUED WITH HEAVY WOOL UNIFORMS.

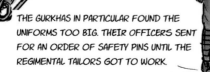

THE GURKHAS IN PARTICULAR FOUND THE UNIFORMS TOO BIG. THEIR OFFICERS SENT FOR AN ORDER OF SAFETY PINS UNTIL THE REGIMENTAL TAILORS GOT TO WORK.

TECHNOLOGY WAS RAPIDLY ADVANCING AND THE TROOPS SAW
MANY NEW MACHINES SUCH AS AEROPLANES.

LOOK MIR - SCIENCE IS A WONDERFUL THING!

THEY WERE ALSO VERY INVENTIVE THEMSELVES, MAKING BOMBS FROM
JAM TINS AND BITS OF SCRAP METAL AND MORTARS FROM DRAINAGE PIPES.

KEEP UP THE GOOD WORK BOYS
WE WILL NEED ALL THE BOMBS
WE CAN MAKE.

MANY INDIAN WORDS ENTERED THE ENGLISH LANGUAGE AT THIS TIME SUCH AS CUSHY MEANING COMFORTABLE.

BACK UP TO THE TRENCHES
THEN MIR - I HOPE IT'S
A CUSHY PART OF THE LINE.

VAUGHAN'S RIFLES COUNTER-ATTACKED THE GERMAN TRENCH.

INTO THEM BOYS!!

THEY ADVANCED DOWN THE TRENCH BOMBING AS THEY WENT, MIR MAST LEADING THE WAY.

GET READY - HERE THEY COME.

ALONG WITH THE GURKHAS, VAUGHAN'S RIFLES FOUGHT BRAVELY. THEY USED FIRE AND MOVEMENT TACTICS THEY HAD DEVELOPED ON THE NORTH WEST FRONTIER TO GREAT EFFECT.

THE BATTLE TURNED INTO A BOMBING CONTEST. THE INDIAN TROOPS HAD THE ADVANTAGE OF DEADLY CRICKET PRACTISE!

EVENTUALLY IT PETERED OUT INTO THE USUAL STALEMATE.
BOTH SIDES EXHAUSTED.

MIR MAST HAD LEAD THE COUNTER ATTACK AND HELPED
RECOVER THE WOUNDED AFTER THE FIGHT. IT HAD BEEN
A REAL TEST FOR THE RIFLES AND THEY PASSED WITH
FLYING COLOURS.

THE RIFLES WERE PULLED OUT OF THE LINE FOR REST AND RECUPERATION.

THE SEPOYS REFLECTED ON THE WAR AND THEIR PART IN IT.

HAVE YOU HEARD THAT TURKEY IS JOINING THE WAR?

ON THE SIDE OF THE ALLEMANDS TOO...

IT IS NOT GOOD TO BE FIGHTING FELLOW MUSLIMS.

I FEAR NONE OF US WILL SURVIVE THESE BATTLES. THE CASUALTIES ARE SO HIGH.

BUT WE TOOK THE SARKARS SALT, MIR - WE HAVE A DUTY TO FULFIL.

INDEED BUT IF I DIE HERE WHO WILL BURY ME WHEN WE ARE ALL DEAD?

*ALLEMANDS = GERMANS, SARKAR = INDIAN GOVERNMENT, TAKING THE SALT = PAYMENT

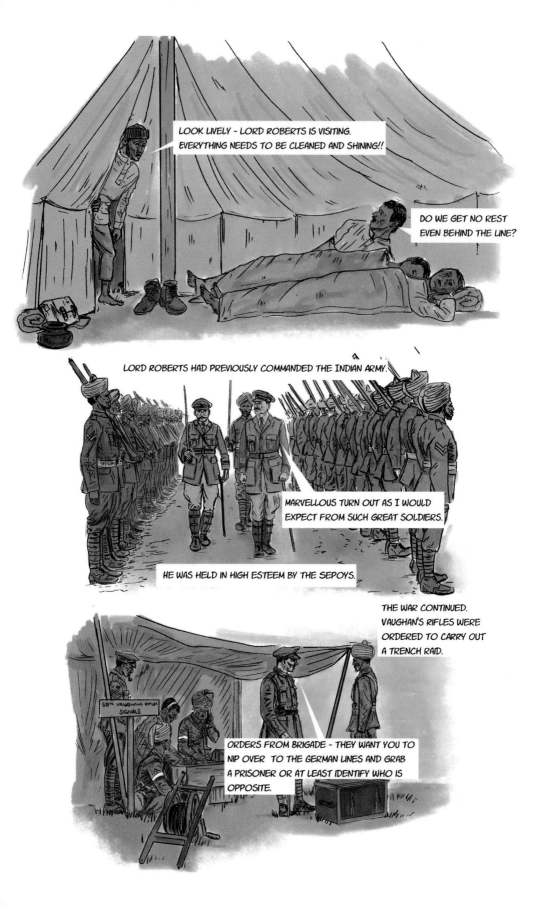

THE INDIAN TROOPS WERE MOVED BACK OUT OF THE LINE TO REST AND RE-EQUIP DURING DECEMBER.

THEY WOULD BE BACK IN THE LINE AGAIN IN JANUARY 1915.

AMONGST THE REINFORCEMENTS AND REPLACEMENTS WAS MIR MASTS BROTHER MIR DAST. HE WAS OLDER AND HAD SERVED LONGER, ALREADY HAVING WON THE INDIAN ORDER OF MERIT (THIRD CLASS) DURING THE 1908 MOHMAND EXPEDITION. HE WAS IN THE 55TH (COKE'S) RIFLES BUT WAS SENT AS A REPLACEMENT TO 57TH WILDE'S RIFLES.

MY BROTHER - AM I GLAD TO SEE YOU BUT WOULD HAVE WARNED YOU NOT TO COME - ITS HELL HERE.

THE SEPOYS KEPT UP WITH NEWS FROM HOME AND THE WIDER WORLD VIA THE PAPERS - THE LITERATE SEPOYS READING THEM OUT FOR THE OTHERS. THAT WINTER THEY LEARNT OF THE HOLY WAR DECLARED BY THE TURKISH SULTAN-CALIPH - THE LEADER OF THE MUSLIM WORLD.

THIS NEWS IS HARD TO BEAR. AS MUSLIMS WE SHOULD NOT BE FIGHTING AGAINST OUR BROTHERS BUT WE HAVE A DUTY AS SOLDIERS...

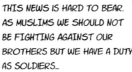

THE ISLAND FORWARD POSITIONS WERE VERY ISOLATED.

THE DUTY OFFICER - LIEUTENANT JOHN TANCRED DID HIS ROUNDS BY NIGHT.

WHEN HE REACHED THE FOREMOST POST HE FINDS IT DESERTED.

WHERE IS EVERYONE?

THEY HAVE ALL DISAPPEARED.

THERE IS NO SIGN OF FIGHT.

THEY MUST HAVE RUNAWAY SIR!

WE MUST GET BACK AND REPORT THIS.

I NEED SOMEONE RELIABLE OUT THERE, JEMADAR MAST, TAKE YOUR SECTION AND HOLD THE POST. I'LL BE BACK TOMORROW NIGHT TO CHECK ON YOU.

YES SIR!

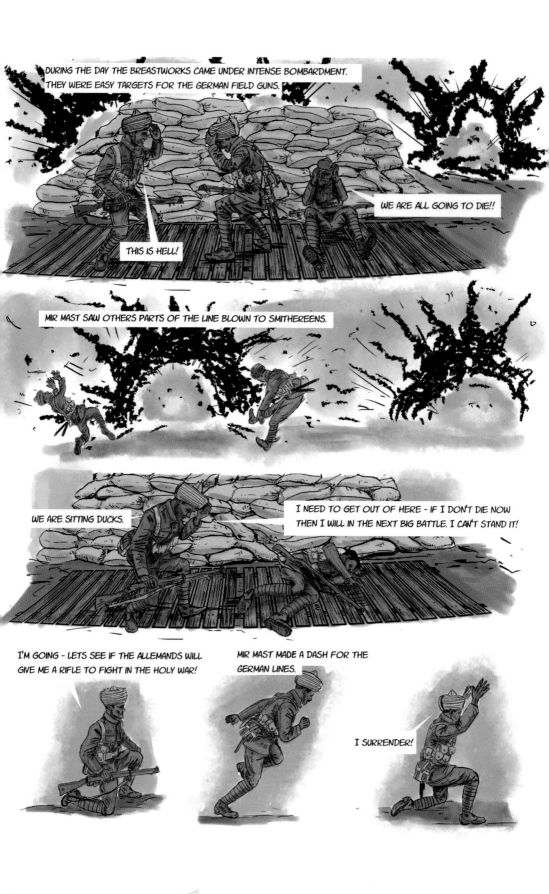

MIR MAST WAS TAKEN PRISONER AND ESCORTED BACK.

HE WAS TREATED WITH SOME SUSPICION.

WHY HAVE YOU SURRENDERED?

I WISH TO HELP IN THE HOLY WAR. YOU PROMISED A RIFLE.

MORE WILL COME IF YOU FULFIL THAT PROMISE!

IN TOTAL FOURTEEN AFRIDIS DISAPPEARED THAT NIGHT. IT'S NOT CLEAR IF IT WAS PLANNED OR THEY JUST TOOK THEIR OPPORTUNITY UNDER THE TERRIBLE BOMBARDMENT.

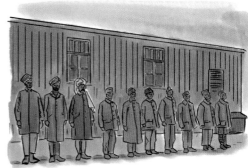

THEY WERE SENT BACK TO A SPECIAL PRISONER OF WAR CAMP WHERE THE GERMANS KEPT ALL CAPTURED COLONIAL TROOPS

WHEN THE OFFICER WENT BACK AGAIN LATER THAT EVENING HE FOUND THE POSITION DESERTED ONCE MORE.

GENERAL WILLCOCKS DECIDED THAT THEY SHOULDN'T OVERREACT AND PLAYED THE INCIDENT DOWN.

THE BRITISH TOOK IMMEDIATE ACTION AND DISARMED SOME OF THE TROOPS THEY FELT UNRELIABLE.

SOME SOLDIERS WERE SENT HOME OR TO OTHER FRONTS.

MIR DAST WAS INFORMED OF HIS BROTHERS ACTIONS.

I'M AFRAID WE HAVE SOME NEWS - YOUR BROTHER HAS DESERTED.

I WILL REMAIN TRUE TO MY SALT SAHIB AND WILL PROVE I AM A LOYAL SOLDIER.

NEAR YPRES FURTHER NORTH IN BELGIUM, EVENTS WERE TAKING A TERRIBLE TURN THAT WOULD ALSO INVOLVE THE INDIAN SEPOYS.

FRENCH COLONIAL TROOPS FROM MOROCCO SAW A STRANGE GREENISH YELLOW CLOUD ROLLING ACROSS NO MANS LAND - GAS!!

TOTALLY UNPREPARED AND DEFENCELESS A GAP OPENED IN THE ALLIED LINE.

THE GERMANS ADVANCED TENTATIVELY WEARING CRUDE GAS MASKS.

THE GERMANS HADN'T EXPECTED MUCH SUCCESS AND WERE NERVOUS OF GASSING THEIR OWN TROOPS'

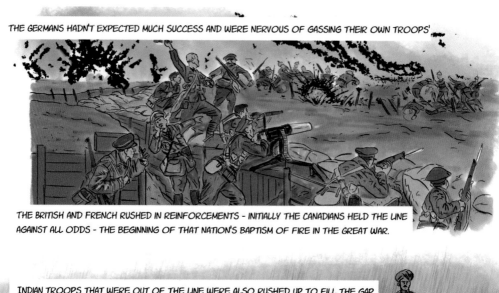

THE BRITISH AND FRENCH RUSHED IN REINFORCEMENTS - INITIALLY THE CANADIANS HELD THE LINE AGAINST ALL ODDS - THE BEGINNING OF THAT NATION'S BAPTISM OF FIRE IN THE GREAT WAR.

INDIAN TROOPS THAT WERE OUT OF THE LINE WERE ALSO RUSHED UP TO FILL THE GAP.

AMONGST THEM, WILDE'S RIFLES MARCHED UP IN THE RAIN.

ALLAH AKBAR!!!

THEY LAUNCHED A DESPERATE COUNTER ATTACK.

IT FAILED IN A HAIL OF RIFLE AND MACHINE GUN FIRE...

HE RESCUED EIGHT BRITISH AND INDIAN OFFICERS WHILST UNDER FIRE FROM THE GERMAN LINES.

AGAIN AND AGAIN HE WENT BACK TO HELP HIS FELLOW SOLDIERS.

HE WAS HIMSELF WOUNDED AND HAD TO BE EVACUATED.

THE FIRST STOP WAS A CASUALTY CLEARING STATION NEAR THE TRENCHES.

THEN BY AMBULANCE TO A HOSPITAL.

HE WAS PUT ON BOARD A SHIP TO ENGLAND.

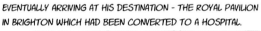

EVENTUALLY ARRIVING AT HIS DESTINATION - THE ROYAL PAVILION IN BRIGHTON WHICH HAD BEEN CONVERTED TO A HOSPITAL.

THE ROYAL PAVILION WAS BUILT BY PRINCE GEORGE IN THE 1800S. QUEEN VICTORIA DISLIKED THE PALACE AND GAVE IT TO THE CITY OF BRIGHTON. IT WAS FELT THE WOUNDED INDIAN TROOPS WOULD FEEL AT HOME THERE AND SO WAS USED AS A HOSPITAL FOR THEM.

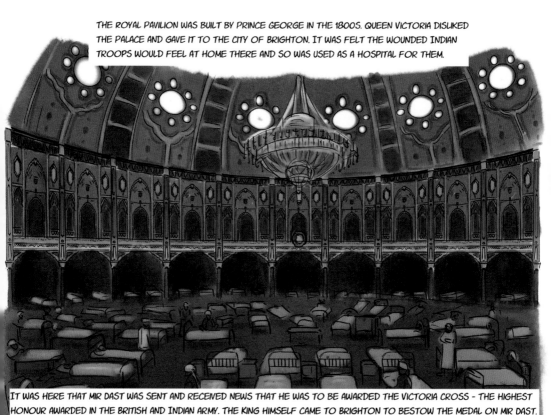

IT WAS HERE THAT MIR DAST WAS SENT AND RECEIVED NEWS THAT HE WAS TO BE AWARDED THE VICTORIA CROSS - THE HIGHEST HONOUR AWARDED IN THE BRITISH AND INDIAN ARMY. THE KING HIMSELF CAME TO BRIGHTON TO BESTOW THE MEDAL ON MIR DAST.

HIS CITATION READ - "FOR MOST CONSPICUOUS BRAVERY AND GREAT ABILITY AT YPRES ON 26TH APRIL 1915, WHEN HE LED HIS PLATOON WITH GREAT GALLANTRY DURING THE ATTACK, AND AFTERWARDS COLLECTED VARIOUS PARTIES OF THE REGIMENT (WHEN NO BRITISH OFFICERS WERE LEFT) AND KEPT THEM UNDER HIS COMMAND UNTIL THE RETIREMENT WAS ORDERED. JEMADAR MIR DAST SUBSEQUENTLY ON THIS DAY DISPLAYED REMARKABLE COURAGE IN HELPING TO CARRY EIGHT BRITISH AND INDIAN OFFICERS INTO SAFETY, WHILST EXPOSED TO VERY HEAVY FIRE."

A WOUND IN HIS LEFT HAND HAD LEFT TWO FINGERS 'POWERLESS', WHILE THE EFFECTS OF THE GAS GAVE HIM GREAT PAIN: 'THE VICTORIA CROSS IS A VERY FINE THING, BUT THIS GAS GIVES ME NO REST. IT HAS DONE FOR ME'. GEORGE V, THE EMPEROR OF INDIA, FORMALLY PRESENTED MIR DAST WITH HIS VC IN THE PAVILION GROUNDS IN LATE AUGUST, WATCHED BY A CROWD OF WOUNDED INDIANS. IN A LETTER HOME MIR DAST WROTE OF HOW 'BY THE GREAT, GREAT, GREAT KINDNESS OF GOD, THE KING WITH HIS ROYAL HAND HAS GIVEN ME THE DECORATION OF THE VICTORIA CROSS … THE DESIRE OF MY HEART IS ACCOMPLISHED'

WHEN THE KING ASKED IF HE HAD ANY REQUEST, MIR DAST URGED 'THAT WHEN A MAN HAS ONCE BEEN WOUNDED, IT IS NOT WELL TO TAKE HIM BACK AGAIN TO THE TRENCHES. FOR NO GOOD WORK WILL BE DONE BY HIS HAND, BUT HE WILL SPOIL OTHERS' ALSO'

TRADITIONALLY, ONCE AN INDIAN SOLDIER HAD BEEN WOUNDED, HE HAD 'DONE HIS BIT', AND THEREFORE SHOULD NOT BE RETURNED TO THE TRENCHES TO RISK DEATH A SECOND TIME AFTER HE HAD RECOVERED. THE MATTER HAD ALREADY FORMED THE SUBJECT OF A PETITION. THE BRITISH AUTHORITIES, GROWING ANXIOUS OVER THE MORALE OF THE INDIAN TROOPS, WERE TO GRANT MIR DAST'S REQUEST.

WHILST AT THE PRISONER OF WAR CAMP MIR MAST HAD BEEN RECRUITED BY THE GERMANS TO HELP
IN A MISSION TO INFLAME A HOLY WAR IN AFGHANISTAN AND ON THE BORDERS OF BRITISH INDIA.

HE WAS THE MAIN INDIAN OFFICER AMONGST A GROUP OF SIX THAT
WHERE TO GO ON THE MISSION. PROMINENT GERMAN MEMBERS OF
THE EXPEDITION WERE OSKAR NIEDERMAYER AND WERNER OTTO VON
HENTIG AS WELL AS OTHER GERMAN OFFICERS.
NIEDERMAYER HAD SERVED IN CONSTANTINOPLE BEFORE THE WAR
AND SPOKE FLUENT PERSIAN AND OTHER REGIONAL LANGUAGES.
A BAVARIAN ARTILLERY OFFICER NIEDERMAYER, HAD TRAVELLED
IN PERSIA AND INDIA IN THE TWO YEARS PRECEDING THE WAR.

TO EVADE BRITISH AND RUSSIAN INTELLIGENCE,
THE GROUP SPLIT UP, BEGINNING THEIR JOURNEYS
ON DIFFERENT DAYS AND SEPARATELY MAKING
THEIR WAY TO CONSTANTINOPLE (ISTANBUL).

AFTER REACHING CONSTANTINOPLE THE GROUP NOW NUMBERING TWENTY PEOPLE ORGANISED
SUPPLIES AND TRANSPORT. THEY SET OFF IN EARLY MAY 1915 CROSSING THE TAURUS MOUNTAINS,
AND THE EUPHRATES RIVER IN FLOOD BEFORE SPLITTING AGAIN INTO GROUPS TO CROSS THE DESERT.

THE GROUP CROSSED THE PERSIAN DESERT
IN FORTY NIGHTS. DYSENTERY AND DELIRIUM
PLAGUED THE PARTY. SOME PERSIAN GUIDES
ATTEMPTED TO DEFECT, AND CAMEL DRIVERS
HAD TO BE CONSTANTLY VIGILANT FOR ROBBERS.

BRITISH AND RUSSIAN SPIES IN PERSIA HAD GOT NEWS OF THE EXPEDITION.

THE BRITISH PATROLS - MOSTLY INDIAN CAVALRY, COVERED THE PERSIAN - AFGHANISTAN BORDER

RUSSIAN COSSACKS PATROLLED FURTHER NORTH.

A GERMAN OFFICER LED A SMALL GROUP INCLUDING SOME OF THE INDIAN SOLDIERS NORTH.

THE RUSSIANS AMBUSHED THEM AND KILLED SOME OF THEIR NUMBER BEFORE THEY COULD FLEE.

IN AUGUST AFTER CROSSING THE BARREN DASHT-E KAVIR DESERT AND NEARLY DYING OF THIRST THEY ENTERED AFGHANISTAN IN THE VICINITY OF HERAT WHERE THEY MADE CONTACT WITH THE AFGHAN AUTHORITIES.

NOW IN KABUL THE MISSION MET WITH OTHER TURKISH OFFICERS AND INDIAN NATIONALISTS SUCH AS MAHENFRA PRATAP.

THE EMIR OF AFGHANISTAN, HABIBULLAH KHAN, GRANTED THEM AN AUDIENCE. THE MEETING LASTED ALL DAY AND ACCORDING TO REPORTS WAS UNCOMFORTABLE AND INCONCLUSIVE.
THE EMIR WAS CAUGHT IN A VULNERABLE POSITION BETWEEN RUSSIA AND BRITISH INDIA. IN THE END THE TALKS PROVED FRUITLESS AS THE EMIR WOULD NOT COMMIT TO WAR.

HABIBULLAH KHAN, EMIR OF AFGHANISTAN.

MIR MAST WAS LEFT TO WANDER THE BEAUTIFUL GARDENS OF KABUL AND CONTEMPLATED WHAT TO DO NEXT.

AT SOME STAGE HE DECIDED TO HEAD HOME TO THE TIRAH REGION (NOW IN MODERN DAY PAKISTAN). HE SLIPPED OFF AND TRAVELLED BACK QUIETLY.

ON REACHING HIS HOME MIR MAST ATTEMPTED TO
RAISE AN ARMY TO REVOLT AGAINST THE BRITISH RULE.

ALTHOUGH HE GATHERED SOME VOLUNTEERS IT WAS ULTIMATELY UNSUCCESSFUL.

THE ELDERS OF THE REGION DID NOT SUPPORT A
REVOLT AND ORDERED MIR MAST TO STOP. THEY
DESTROYED HIS HOUSE AND HE WAS SENT TO LIVE
WITH HIS BROTHER MIR DAST WHO HAD RETURNED
A HERO WITH HIS AWARD OF THE VICTORIA CROSS.
IT WAS RUMOURED THE KAISER HAD AWARDED MIR
MAST THE IRON CROSS BUT THERE IS NO RECORD
OF THIS.

MIR MAST IS BELIEVED TO HAVE DIED
IN THE FLU EPIDEMIC OF 1918.

MIR DAST LIVED UNTIL 1945 BUT
WOUNDS CONSTANTLY CAUSED HIM
PAIN.

THE TWO BROTHERS HAD VERY DIFFERENT
STORIES TO TELL AND THEY TOOK DIFFERING
PATHS. EACH MADE HIS OWN WAY AS BEST AS HE
COULD, ACCORDING TO THEIR OWN CONVICTIONS
IN A WORLD WAR THAT CAUSED SO MUCH PAIN
AND SUFFERING AND TO THIS DAY RESULTS IN
STRIFE AND CONFLICT

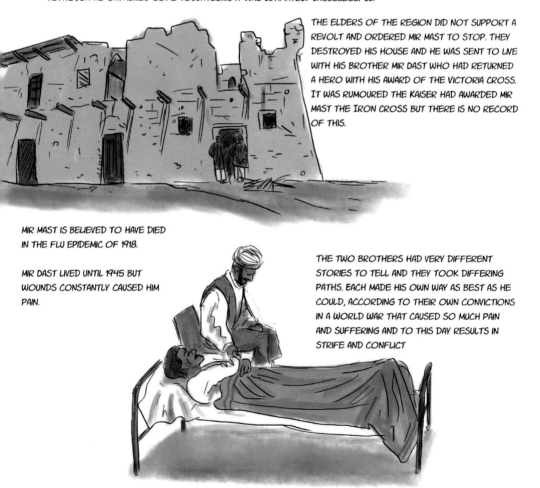

I FIRST READ THE STORY OF THE TWO BROTHERS IN DAVID OLUSOGA'S EXCELLENT BOOK - THE WORLDS WAR. THEY MUST HAVE PERSONIFIED SO MANY OF THE INDIAN SOLDIERS' THOUGHTS AND SPLIT LOYALTIES. OVER ONE MILLION INDIAN TROOPS SERVED OVERSEAS, OF WHOM 62,000 DIED AND ANOTHER 67,000 WERE WOUNDED. IN TOTAL AT LEAST 74,187 INDIAN SOLDIERS DIED DURING THE WAR. EVENTUALLY IT WOULD TAKE ANOTHER WORLD WAR BEFORE INDIA GAINED INDEPENDENCE FROM BRITAIN. I LIVE IN BRIGHTON AND OFTEN VISIT THE CHATTRI MEMORIAL WHERE THE HINDU AND SIKH SOLDIERS WHO DIED IN THE HOSPITALS WERE BURNT IN A FUNERAL PYRE. THE MUSLIMS WERE BURIED IN A CEMETERY IN WOKING NEARBY.

THE INSCRIPTION ON THE CHATTRI READS:
TO THE MEMORY OF ALL INDIAN SOLDIERS WHO GAVE THEIR LIVES FOR THE KING-EMPEROR IN THE GREAT WAR, THIS MONUMENT, ERECTED ON THE SITE OF THE FUNERAL PYRE WHERE HINDUS AND SIKHS WHO DIED IN HOSPITAL AT BRIGHTON PASSED THROUGH THE FIRE, IS IN GRATEFUL ADMIRATION AND BROTHERLY LOVE DEDICATED.

I THINK OF IT AS A MEMORIAL TO ALL WHO SERVED ON ALL SIDES NO MATTER THE PATH THEY TOOK.

AN INFANTRY OFFICER WINS THE MILITARY CROSS

How Siegfried Sassoon was awarded the MC

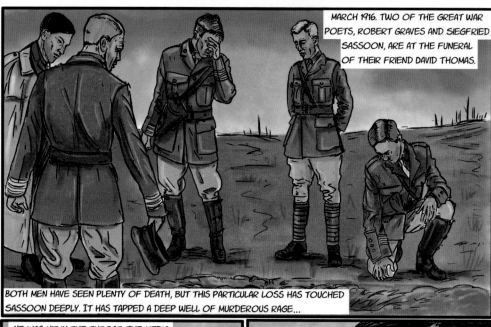

MARCH 1916. TWO OF THE GREAT WAR POETS, ROBERT GRAVES AND SIEGFRIED SASSOON, ARE AT THE FUNERAL OF THEIR FRIEND DAVID THOMAS.

BOTH MEN HAVE SEEN PLENTY OF DEATH, BUT THIS PARTICULAR LOSS HAS TOUCHED SASSOON DEEPLY. IT HAS TAPPED A DEEP WELL OF MURDEROUS RAGE...

HE WAS HIT IN THE THROAT. THE MEDIC TOLD HIM TO LIE ABSOLUTELY STILL.

BUT HE REACHED FOR A LETTER TO SEND HOME IN HIS TUNIC POCKET. THAT GESTURE KILLED HIM.

I SHAN'T FORGIVE THIS, GRAVES.

I SHALL PERSONALLY STRANGLE EVERY BOCHE I CAN LAY MY HANDS ON.

TO TRY TO FORGET, SASSOON OFTEN TOOK THE TRANSPORT HORSES OUT. GALLOPING ACROSS THE PICARDY COUNTRYSIDE WHICH REMINDED HIM OF HIS YOUTH, FOX HUNTING ON THE KENT WEALD.

OR VOLUNTEERING FOR DANGEROUS PATROLS IN NO MANS LAND, WANTING TO WREAK REVENGE.

BACK AT BATTALION HQ, SASSOON'S BLOODLUST WAS NOTED BY HIS SUPERIORS.

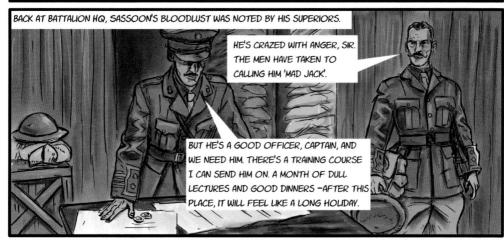

HE'S CRAZED WITH ANGER, SIR. THE MEN HAVE TAKEN TO CALLING HIM 'MAD JACK'.

BUT HE'S A GOOD OFFICER, CAPTAIN, AND WE NEED HIM. THERE'S A TRAINING COURSE I CAN SEND HIM ON. A MONTH OF DULL LECTURES AND GOOD DINNERS —AFTER THIS PLACE, IT WILL FEEL LIKE A LONG HOLIDAY.

THE COURSE WAS AT THE BRITISH ARMY SCHOOL IN FLEXICOURT.

SASSOON RESTED, AND HE WROTE. BUT THE DESIRE FOR REVENGE DID NOT ABATE — IF ANYTHING IT BURNED MORE BRIGHTLY WEEK ON WEEK.

THIS HERE IS YOUR BEST FRIEND!

STICK IT IN THE HUNS GUTS!!

HE WROTE THE POEM 'THE KISS' AFTER ATTENDING THE LECTURE 'THE SPIRIT OF THE BAYONET' BY MAJOR CAMPBELL.

"TO THESE I TURN, IN THESE I TRUST— BROTHER LEAD AND SISTER STEEL. TO HIS BLIND POWER I MAKE APPEAL, I GUARD HER BEAUTY CLEAN FROM RUST."

TWIST AND DRIVE IT IN!

USE YOUR BOOT ON HIM IF IT DOESN'T COME OUT.

SIEGFRIED RETURNS TO BILLETS IN MORLANCOURT WHEN THE COURSE FINISHES.

AH, KANGA IS BACK. WELCOME HOME OLD CHAP!

YOU'RE BACK IN TIME FOR THE RAID. THE COLONEL WANTS ME TO LEAD IT.

KANGA IS SASSOON'S NICKNAME.

I WANT TO GO ON THE RAID. IT'S MY CHANCE TO GET REVENGE FOR DAVID.

I'LL ASK THE COLONEL IF I CAN JOIN THE RAID....

SASSOON DECIDES TO VISIT HIS FRIEND, QUARTERMASTER JOE DOTTRILL, AND GET NEWS ON THE RAID.

THEY BECAME GOOD FRIENDS WHEN SASSOON WAS TRANSPORT OFFICER.

YOU DON'T WANT TO GET YOURSELF INVOLVED IN THE RAID. IT'S A BADDISH PLACE FOR A SHOW LIKE THAT...

SASSOON'S COMPANY MOVE UP THE LINE THAT NIGHT FOR THEIR TOUR OF THE TRENCHES.

IN THE DUGOUT...

WHO ARE YOU WRITING TO KANGA?

MY MOTHER - I PLAN TO GO ON THE RAID. CAN YOU POST IT FOR ME IF ANYTHING HAPPENS?

THE NEXT DAY WAS THE DATE FOR THE RAID, SASSOON REPORTED TO BATTALION HQ AT MAPLE REDOUBT.

THERE HE SAW THE RAIDERS MAKING PREPARATIONS.

THEIR BLACKENED FACES REMINDED HIM OF MINSTRELS BUT THEY HELD CLUBS INSTEAD OF BANJOS.

SIR, I'D LIKE TO LEAD THE RAID.

SORRY - NO. YOU ARE NEEDED TO COUNT THE MEN OUT AND BACK IN AGAIN.

THE RAIDING PARTY OF TWENTY MEN SETS OFF FOR THE FRONT IN THE POURING RAIN.

A SOLDIER WITH A RED LIGHT LEADS THE WAY INTO THE COMMUNICATION TRENCH.

THE TROOPS SET UP LADDERS TO HELP THE RAIDERS IN AND OUT OF THE TRENCHES.

SENTRIES WATCH THEM DISAPPEAR INTO THE DARK OF NO MAN'S LAND.

LT MANSFIELD AND CORPORAL O'BRIEN LEAD THE WAY AND MARK THE ROUTE WITH LIME.

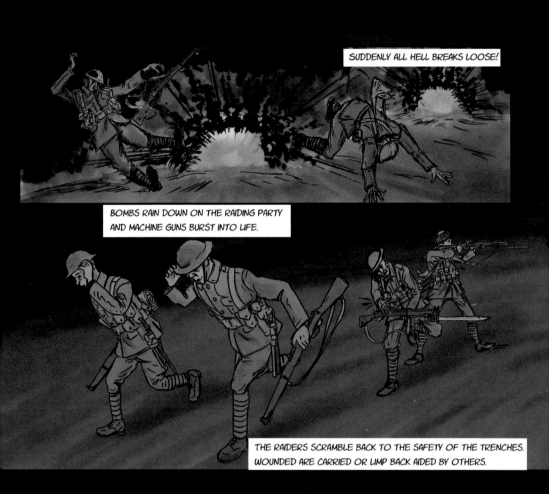

SUDDENLY ALL HELL BREAKS LOOSE!

BOMBS RAIN DOWN ON THE RAIDING PARTY AND MACHINE GUNS BURST INTO LIFE.

THE RAIDERS SCRAMBLE BACK TO THE SAFETY OF THE TRENCHES. WOUNDED ARE CARRIED OR LIMP BACK AIDED BY OTHERS.

SASSOON COUNTED THEM BACK IN AND REALISED THAT A FEW HADN'T MADE IT

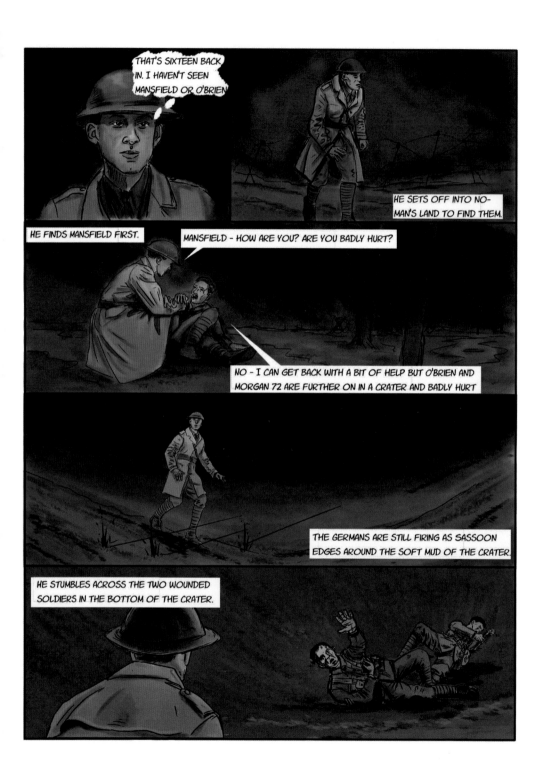

SASSOON IS AWARDED THE MILITARY CROSS. HIS CITATION READS:
FOR CONSPICUOUS GALLANTRY DURING A RAID ON THE ENEMY'S TRENCHES.
HE REMAINED FOR ONE AND A HALF HOURS UNDER RIFLE AND BOMB FIRE
COLLECTING AND BRINGING IN OUR WOUNDED. OWING TO HIS COURAGE AND
DETERMINATION ALL THE KILLED AND WOUNDED WERE BROUGHT IN.

OF THE RAIDING PARTY TWO WERE KILLED AND TEN
WOUNDED CORPORAL O'BRIEN IS BURIED IN CITADEL NEW
MILITARY CEMETERY, FRICOURT PLOT 3, ROW F, GRAVE 17

DULCE ET DECORUM EST

WILFRED OWEN MC WAS AN ENGLISH POET AND SOLDIER. HE WAS ONE OF THE LEADING POETS OF THE FIRST WORLD WAR. HIS WAR POETRY ON THE HORRORS OF TRENCHES AND GAS WARFARE WAS MUCH INFLUENCED BY HIS MENTOR SIEGFRIED SASSOON. MOST OF WHICH WERE PUBLISHED POSTHUMOUSLY "DULCE ET DECORUM EST" IS PROBABLY HIS MOST WELL KNOWN WORK.

OWEN WAS KILLED IN ACTION ON 4 NOVEMBER 1918, A WEEK BEFORE THE WAR'S END, AT THE AGE OF 25.

Dulce et Decorum Est

By Wilfred Owen

Bent double, like old beggars under sacks,

Knock-kneed, coughing like hags, we cursed through sludge,

Till on the haunting flares we turned our backs,
And towards our distant rest began to trudge.

Men marched asleep.
Many had lost their boots,
But limped on, blood-shod.
All went lame; all blind;

Drunk with fatigue; deaf even to the hoots
Of gas-shells dropping softly behind.

Gas! GAS! Quick, boys! —

—An ecstasy of fumbling
Fitting the clumsy helmets just in time,

But someone still was yelling out and stumbling

And flound'ring like a man in fire or lime. —

Dim through the misty panes
and thick green light,

As under a green sea, I saw him drowning.

In all my dreams before my helpless sight,

He plunges at me, guttering,
choking, drowning.

If in some smothering dreams,
you too could pace
Behind the wagon that we flung him in ,

And watch the white eyes
writhing in his face,

His hanging face,
like a devil's sick of sin

If you could hear, at every jolt, the blood
Come gargling from the froth-corrupted lungs,

Obscene as cancer, bitter as the cud

Of vile, incurable sores on innocent tongues,—
My friend, you would not tell with such high zest

To children ardent for some desperate glory,

The old Lie: Dulce et decorum est
Pro patria mori.

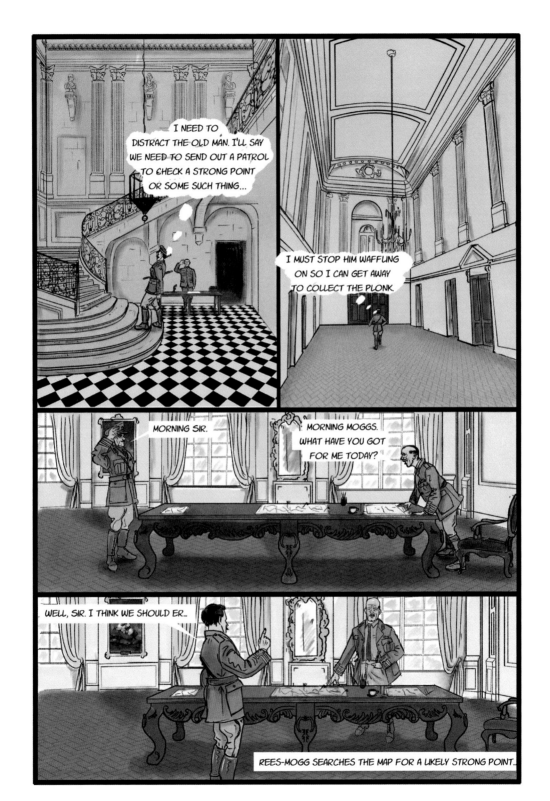

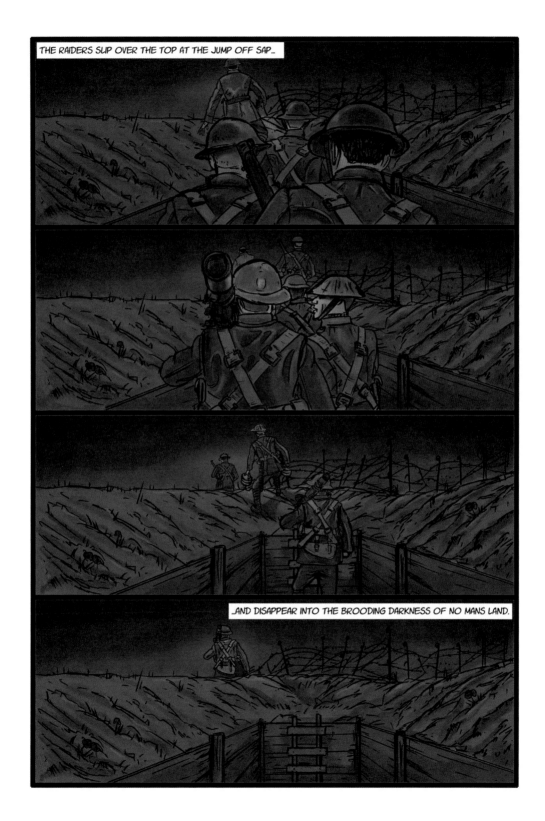

GLASS EYE ⊙ WARNES

THIS IS THE STORY OF SQUADRON LEADER GEOFFREY WARNES, THE MOST SHORT SIGHTED PILOT IN THE RAF.

HE WAS A YORKSHIREMAN – BORN IN LEEDS IN 1914. HE LEFT SCHOOL AT SIXTEEN AND WORKED AS AN OFFICE CLERK. IT WAS A DULL JOB FOR SURE – BUT WARNES HAD OTHER PASSIONS. HE WAS, FOR ONE THING, A FINE RUGBY PLAYER, TURNING OUT EACH WEEK FOR HEADINGLEY RFC. AND HE LONGED TO FLY. IN THE 1930S WARNES TOOK LESSONS AT THE YORKSHIRE AEROPLANE CLUB WHERE HIS TEACHER WAS GINGER LACY, A FUTURE BATTLE OF BRITAIN ACE.

WAR WAS DECLARED IN SEPTEMBER 1939.

WORLD WAR DECLARED (OFFICIAL)

GEOFF VOLUNTEERS FOR THE RAF, BUT WAS REJECTED BECAUSE HE WORE GLASSES.

HE PERSISTED AND WAS EVENTUALLY ACCEPTED - BUT FOR GROUND DUTIES ONLY.

GEOFF DIDN'T SETTLE FOR THAT. HE WAS COMMISSIONED AS AN ACTING PILOT OFFICER AND POSTED TO FRANCE IN APRIL 1940.

...JUST IN TIME FOR THE GERMAN INVASION. THIS WAS BLITZKRIEG. FAST-MOVING ARMOUR, SUPPORTED BY DIVE BOMBERS, SMASHED THROUGH THE ALLIED DEFENCES...

...FRENCH AND BRITISH ARMIES WERE FORCED TO RETREAT TOWARDS THE SEA.

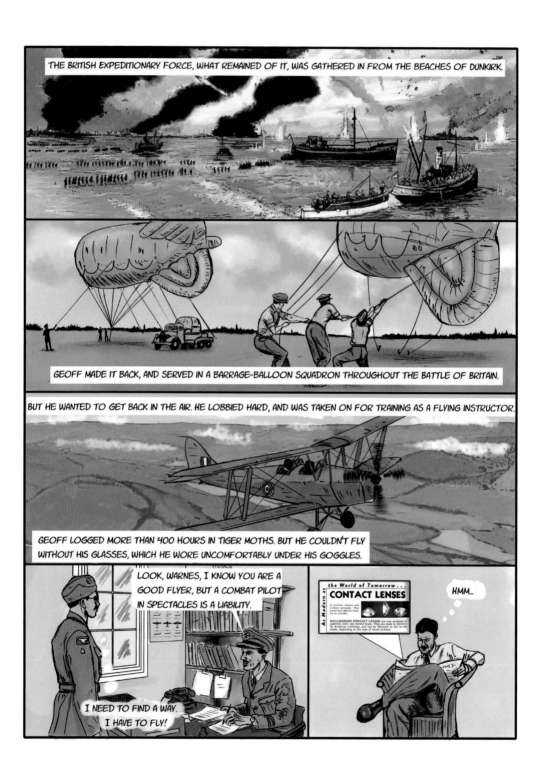

THE WINTER OF 1941 WAS QUIET FOR GEOFF. ENDLESS FOG KEPT THE WHIRLWINDS GROUNDED.

THE WAR, LIKE THE WEATHER, WARMED UP IN SPRING...

...PATROLS AND OPERATIONS OVER FRANCE RESUMED.

THE FOUR 20MM NOSE-CANNONS WERE STRIPPED AND REARMED.

THE WHIRLWINDS WERE NOW FITTED WITH 250LB BOMBS.

BUT NO MORE WHIRLWINDS WERE MANUFACTURED AFTER 1942. THIS WAS BECAUSE THE AIRCRAFT WAS THOUGHT BY SOME TO HAVE DESIGN FAULTS. BUT THE MEN THAT ACTUALLY FLEW THE PLANE, OR SERVED IN THE RAF'S TWO SQUADRONS, HAD ABSOLUTE CONFIDENCE IN THE WHIRLWIND.

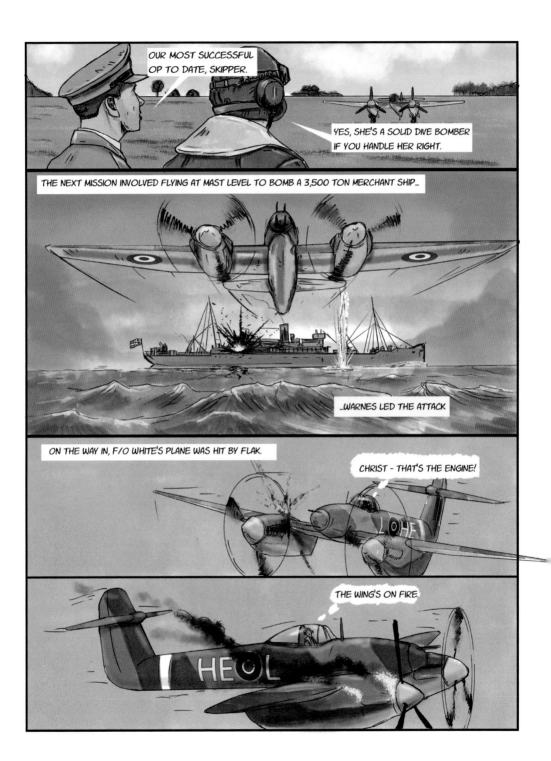

IN JUNE 1943 GEOFF IS AWARDED THE DISTINGUISHED SERVICE ORDER.

STRAIGHT AFTERWARDS HE LEAVES THE SQUADRON. HIS NEW POSTING IS TO NO. 10 GROUP.

HERE GEOFF WORKS IN THE CONTROL ROOMS GUIDING AEROPLANES TO THEIR TARGETS.

MEANWHILE THE WESTLAND WHIRLWINDS ARE TAKEN OUT OF COMMISSION AND REPLACED WITH HAWKER TYPHOONS (TIFFYS).

NO.10 GROUPS TURNS OUT TO BE A SHORT POSTING. SIX MONTHS LATER, GEOFF IS BACK WITH 263 SQUADRON.

WELCOME BACK SKIPPER.

13TH FEBRUARY 1944. A SWEEP OF CHARTRES-MONDESIR CONCENTRATING ON THE CHARTRES AIRFIELD.

F/L RACINE STRAFED FIVE MESSERSCHMITT! 109S AS THEY REFUELLED. THREE WERE DESTROYED ON THE GROUND.

ONE OF THEM MANAGED TO TAKE OFF. GEOFF GAVE CHASE.

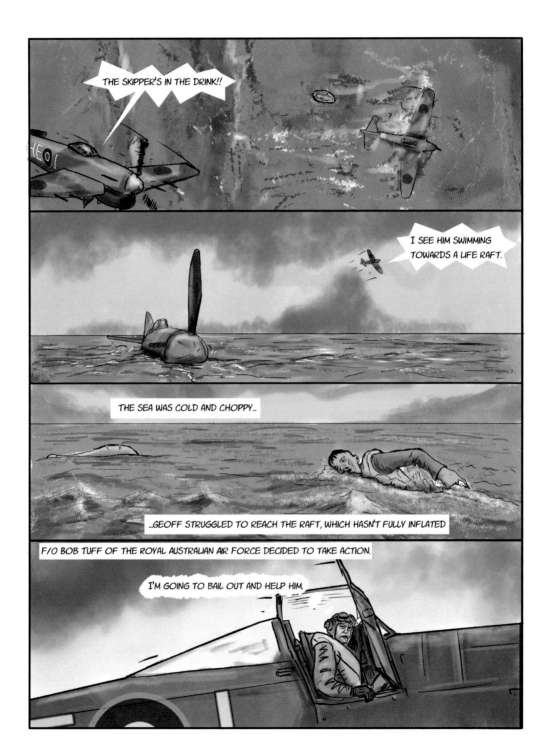

THE SQUADRON RECORDS ALSO HAVE THIS TO SAY ABOUT GEOFFREY BERRINGTON WARNES DSO DFC,
- THE FIRST RAF PILOT TO WEAR CONTACT LENSES: 'HE WAS A STRICT DISCIPLINARIAN WHO COMBINED
A FIERCE AND FORTHRIGHT MANNER WITH PERSONAL KINDNESS; A COMMANDER WHO NEVER LEFT THE
LEAST DOUBT ABOUT WHAT HE WANTED AND WHO CONSISTENTLY OBTAINED THESE QUALITIES BECAUSE
HE HIMSELF CONSISTENTLY DISPLAYED THEM: HE HIMSELF DID EVEN MORE THAN HE REQUIRED OF OTHERS.
S/LDR WARNES MAY HAVE SOME PLACE IN THE HISTORY OF THE WAR AS THE CREATOR OF MEDIUM-LEVEL
DIVE BOMBING BY FIGHTER-BOMBERS. HIS NOTES ON SHIPPING ATTACKS WERE ADOPTED AS A FIGHTER
COMMAND TACTICAL MEMORANDUM.'
I HAVE KNOWN ABOUT WARNES ALL MY LIFE. HE WAS MY GRANDFATHER'S COUSIN, AND GODFATHER TO
MY MOTHER. GRANDAD WAS EXTREMELY PROUD OF HIS COUSIN, AND OFTEN TOLD HIS STORY. HE REFERRED
TO GEOFF AS 'CAT'S EYES', BUT THAT SEEMS TO BE A MIS-RECOLLECTION. ALL THE EVIDENCE SAYS THAT
SQUADRON LEADER WARNES WAS KNOWN TO HIS COMRADES, AFFECTIONATELY, AS 'GLASS EYES'.

GEOFF WARNES DSO DFC 1916-1944

Tim Cutherall

THE FOLLOWING PAGES SHOWCASE A NUMBER OF ILLUSTRATIONS
I HAVE PRODUCE OVER THE YEARS. THEY ARE MOSTLY DIGITAL
AND COVER A RANGE OF SUBJECTS. THE FIRST ONES ON THIS
PAGE ARE ALL WWI AND TEND TO SHOW INDIVIDUAL SOLDIERS. THE
HIGHLAND ON THE RIGHT IS ONE OF MY FIRST ATTEMPTS USING
PHOTOSHOP. THE REFERENCES COME FROM ORIGINAL PHOTOS,
RE-ENACTORS OR FILMS.

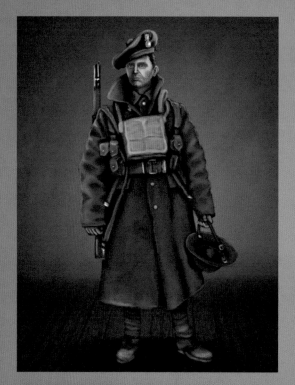

GERMAN STORMTROOPERS
(STOSSTRUPPEN) ARE VERY
DISTINCT AND GREAT TO
ILLUSTRATE. MOST OF THESE
ARE BASED ON PHOTOS BY
RE-ENACTORS MAINLY POSTED
ON INSTAGRAM

PAINTING FROM REFERENCE THAT ISN'T
ORIGINAL MEANS IF YOU AREN'T CAREFUL
YOU CAN MAKE HISTORIC ERRORS
THE SMG'S IN THESE PAINTINGS HAVE
THE WRONG AMMO CLIP - IT SHOULD BE
THE SNAIL SHAPE HOLDER. SOMETIMES
I DON'T NOTICE THIS UNTIL POINTED OUT...

I DO EXPERIMENT WITH VARIOUS TECHNIQUES AND STYLES - HERE ARE SOME OF MY ' DIGITAL PENCIL' SKETCHES. THE INDIAN LANCERS ARE HOWEVER DRAWN TRADITIONALLY WITH PEN. THE IMAGE ABOVE IS AN ATTEMPT TO GIVE DEPTH AND LAYERING TO THE PICTURE.

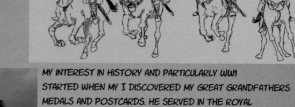

MY INTEREST IN HISTORY AND PARTICULARLY WW1 STARTED WHEN MY I DISCOVERED MY GREAT GRANDFATHERS MEDALS AND POSTCARDS. HE SERVED IN THE ROYAL ENGINEERS AS A SAPPER.

ANOTHER INFLUENCE WAS 'CHARLEY'S WAR' IN BATTLE ACTION COMIC. ITS AVAILABLE NOW PUBLISHED IN A COLLECTION - GET A COPY! WE STUDIED WILFRED OWEN AT SCHOOL AND HE WAS THE ONLY REASON I PASSED ENGLISH LITERATURE. FOLLOWING ON FROM HIS POETRY I DISCOVERED SASSOON, GRAVES, BLUNDEN ETC. I HAVE QUITE A COLLECTION OF MEMOIRS NOW. I'D MUCH RATHER READ A MEMOIR THAN A HISTORY AS THE HUMAN ASPECT IS OF MOST INTEREST TO ME.

HERE ARE SOME MORE ATTEMPTS AT DIFFERENT STYLES. THE BLACK AND WHITE PICTURE IS TRYING TO REPRODUCE THE OLD SCRATCH PADS WE HAD AT SCHOOL

THE BOTTOM PICTURE IS BASED ON A PAINTING BY JOHN NASH. HE WAS AN OFFICIAL ARTIST IN WW1 AND SERVED ON THE WESTERN FRONT. I SAW THE ORIGINAL PAINTING AT AN EXHIBITION IN THE TOWNER GALLERY IN EASTBOURNE. IT DEPICTS AN ACTUAL ATTACK IN WHICH HE TOOK PART.

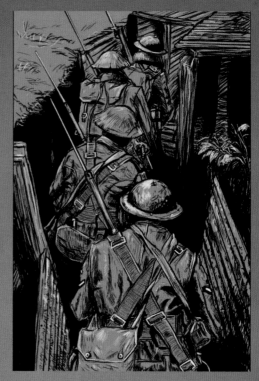

WW2 IS ALSO A PERIOD OF HISTORY I'M
INTERESTED IN. I GREW UP WITH MANY
RELATIVES AND FRIENDS WHO HAD LIVED
THROUGH WW2 AND MY GRANDFATHER
IN PARTICULAR TOLD ME AND MY BROTHERS
STORIES OF THOSE TIMES - ONE OF WHICH
IS IN THE BOOK. AGAIN I HAVE A RANGE OF
SUBJECTS AND REFERENCES

THE PICTURE ABOVE WAS COMMISSIONED BY AN
INSTAGRAM FOLLOWER WHOSE RELATIVE HAD BEEN IN
A CAMP - WE MUST NOT FORGET THE HORRORS WHAT
HUMAN BEINGS ARE CAPABLE OF

I DO TEND TO DRAW ALLIED SUBJECTS AS THIS IS
WHERE MY INTERESTS LAY. I'M VERY INTERESTED IN
THE EXPERIENCE OF COMMONWEALTH AND COLONIAL
SOLDIERS IN BOTH WORLD WARS. IT HAS
BEEN A STORY THAT HAS INCREASING GARNERED
INTEREST AND THERE HAVE BEEN SOME EXCELLENT
BOOKS. I'M DRAWN TO THE PRIVATE, MOSTLY WORKING
CLASS ACCOUNTS AND EXPERIENCE TOO AND HOW
ORDINARY PEOPLE DEALT WITH SUCH A CATACLYSM
AS A WORLD WAR

MORE RECENT CONFLICTS ARE SUBJECTS
TOO. GROWING UP IN THE 1970S AND 80S
THERE WERE A LOT OF FILMS AND BOOKS
ABOUT THE VIETNAM WAR. I'VE TRIED TO READ
ABOUT BOTH SIDES OF THE WAR AND
THE CIVILIAN EXPERIENCE. THERE HAS
BEEN THE EXCELLENT KEN BURNS
DOCUMENTARY RECENTLY WHICH HAD
CONTRIBUTIONS FROM ALL INVOLVED.

I HAVE NO PERSONAL EXPERIENCE OF WAR
IT APPEARS TO ME HORRIFIC AND BEYOND
COMPREHENSION YET I AM FASCINATED BY
THE EXPERIENCES OF THOSE INVOLVED AND
CAUGHT UP IN CONFLICT. AS I LIKE TO DRAW
I FIND THEY TEND TO BE MY SUBJECT.

AND FINALLY A BIT OF TOLKIEN INSPIRED ART.
I HAVE READ LORD OF THE RINGS AND THE HOBBIT
NUMEROUS TIMES. I GREW UP IN THE ENGLISH
MIDLANDS AS DID TOLKIEN . HE SERVED IN WW1 AS
AN OFFICER AND THAT EXPERIENCE FEED INTO HIS
WRITING. A BIT OFCOLOUR TO FINISH WITH.

I HOPE YOU HAVE ENJOYED MY
FIRST GRAPHIC NOVEL